Francis Wayland Campbell

The War of 1812-13-14

Between Great Britain and the United States

Francis Wayland Campbell

The War of 1812-13-14
Between Great Britain and the United States

ISBN/EAN: 9783337115838

Printed in Europe, USA, Canada, Australia, Japan

Cover: Foto ©ninafisch / pixelio.de

More available books at **www.hansebooks.com**

THE

War of 1812 = 13 = 14

BETWEEN

Great Britain and the United States

❧ ❧

A LECTURE DELIVERED

at the

Montreal Military Institute

and before the

Numismatic and Antiquarian Society of Montreal

In February 1899

BY

FRANCIS WAYLAND CAMPBELL

M. A., M. D., L. R. C. P. London, D. C. L.
Deputy Surgeon General,
late Royal Regiment Canadian Infantry

❧

MONTREAL

Alph. Pelletier, Printer, 36 St. Lawrence Street

1899

THE
War of 1812 = 13 = 14

BETWEEN

Great Britain and the United States

❧ ❧

A LECTURE DELIVERED

at the

Montreal Military Institute

and before the

Numismatic and Antiquarian Society of Montreal

In February 1899

BY

FRANCIS WAYLAND CAMPBELL

M. A., M. D., L. R. C. P. London, D. C. L.
Deputy Surgeon General,
late Royal Regiment Canadian Infantry

❧

MONTREAL
Alph. Pelletier, Printer, 36 St. Lawrence Street
1899

THE WAR OF 1812-13-14

ঙ ঙ

SCARCELY a generation had passed away, since the prolonged struggle of the American revolution had ended, when there arose complications, as a result of the struggle which Great Britain had been carrying on for the liberties of Europe. The sources of the war of 1812 are clearly traceable to the events of the preceeding century. Sparks of hostility had remained smouldering between Britain and her revolted Colonies ; and the mother country had possibly not yet entirely forgiven them, or got over the accrimony of the separation. Among a numerous class in the United States there existed a latent and easily excited hatred of everything British. In Canada, the English settlers, consisted chiefly of old British soldiers or United Empire Loyalists, who had left comfortable homesteads in the United States—to make in Canada new homes under the folds of the Union Jack they loved so well. An animosity—the more bitter because the countries were so close—also sprang up between the two countries. This asperity was of course much aggravated by the means which Great Britain took for her protection while fighting Napoleon almost single handed. The paper blocades of 1806 and 1807 by which she and France respectively placed the whole coast of the other, under a " constructive blocade " bore especially hard on the United States, whose marine at this period had almost monopolised the carrying trade of the world. Britain had not only exercised its right of search, but it asserted the right to seize English seamen found on American vessels, so that American sailors were often impressed into the British fleet. The irritation which this caused was kindled into a flame by the arbitrary action of a British Commander. Acting under orders of Vice Admiral Berkeley, Captain Humphries of H. M. S. *Leopard* overhauled the United States frigate *Chesapeake,* and demanded the surrender of alleged deserters. The demand being refused, a broad side compelled the *Chesapeake* to strike her colors and surrender the deserters. This act was at once disavowed by the British Government, before a word of remonstrance from the United States could reach it. The Captain was recalled, the Admiral superseeded and an official note handed the United States declairing right of search when applied to vessels of war extended only to requisition, and was not to be carried by force. Without waiting to see what action Britain would take, the United States, excluded British ships from all American ports. This had a most injurious effect on American trade, especially in New England. A year later this embargo was exchanged for an act of non-intercourse with France and England only. They had no means of enforcing this, so it was withdrawn but they maintained a standing offer that if either power would repeal its edicts, it would suspend commerce with the other. Napoleon seeing his opportunity to checkmate Britain accepted the offer. In February 1811 the United States declared all intercourse with Great Britain and her dependencies at an end. In May 1811 the U.S. frigate *President,* provoked an encounter with the British sloop *Little Belt,* and shot her to pieces. The American Captain was tried by Court Martial and acquitted amid national exultation, Great Britain accepting the official declaration disavowing hostile intention. In November 1811 the President appealed to the nation for the " sinews of war." A large class of the American people, were full of sanguine ' hope of an easy conquest of Canada. It was presumed that political troubles and grievances, connected with the Imperial executive, had so far undermined Canadian loyalty, that the Colonists would interpose, slight resistance to an American invasion. It was known that Bonaparte was desirous of wresting from Britain the New France of the early French Colonists. It was at this time believed that Napoleon would become sole master of Europe, and that the United States by joining hands with him, would divide with him — the empire of the world. Britain, then almost

alone contending against the usurper, it was felt
would neither have the leisure or the power to
defend Canada. Great Britain felt that a junction
between the United States and Napoleon, meant
ruin to English industry — so that after some delay
caused by a ministerial crisis — the obnoxious orders
were repealed on the 23rd of June. The news did not
reach the United States for some weeks, and it came
too late, for on the 18th of June 1812, the American
Congress declared war with Great Britain. Even if
the news had been received in time it is doubted if it
would have averted war, so stong was the feeling of
the majority of the people for it. The step however
was not unopposed. Virginia strongly denounced
the invasion of Canada, and the proposal to seduce
Canadians from their loyalty, and as a prominent
American stateman expressed it "converting them
into traitors, as a preperation for making them good
American citizens." The New England states also
strongly opposed the war, and Boston displayed her
flags at half mast, as a token of mourning, while a
mass meeting passed resolutions, protesting against
the war. Let us for a moment see how the two countries stood as regards population, from which to draw
the required men. The population of the United
States was 8,000,000, while Canada numbered but
300,000. From the Detroit river to Halifax, there
were scattered British regulars, numbering all told
4,500. Upper Canada, now Ontario, where the bulk
of the fighting occurred, had only a population of
little more than 30,000. In the brief time offered by

a lecture it is of course impossible to follow all the
events what took place, in a war which covered nearly
three years. I am therefore compelled to notice only
the principal events. In Canada the inpending storm
had long been dreaded. General Brock who besides
being commander, was administrator of the Government in Upper Canada, had not been slow in reading
the signs of the times, and so far as he could, taking
measures for defence. Great Britain, harassed as she
was with her European war had treated the representa-
tions of the exposed condition of Canada with an unfortunate lack of efficient response. Canada with its
magnificent distances and scattered population could
scarcely have been less prepared for war or worse
equipped for defence. It is not strange that at first there
was some despondency, when she found herself
launched into a war with her powerful neighbor.
But the true British spirit still existed in the Canadian people, many of whom had already sacrificed
much for their love for the old flag. Troops of volunteers poured into all the garrison towns, many
being obliged to retire for lack of arms to equip them.
The news of the declaration of war first reached
Canada, at Montreal through a private channel, the
British Minister at Washington not having taken
efficient means to have it reach the authorities in
Canada. The moment it was known, General Brock
took prompt measures. He established his head
quarters at Fort George on the Niagara river, asked
for reinforcements from Lower Canada (which could
not be granted till reinforcement arrived from Great

Britain) appointed a day of prayer and fasting in recognition of the impending crisis, looked to the frontier forts and outposts and paid special attention to securing the co-operation of the Indians, and the equipment and drilling of the militia. As I have already said, there was a great scarcity of arms, also clothing and shoes which could not be provided for in the country. As to weapons it is said some of the Militia, temporarily supplied themselves from their implements of husbandry. On the 11th of July, General Hull with 1500 men, crossed into Canada from Detroit. At Sandwich he issued a proclamation, offering the Canadian people in exchange for the tyranny under which they were suffering " the invaluable blessings of civil, political and religious liberty. " From Fort George, Brock issued a counter proclamation, reminding them of their prosperity under British rule, and assuring them that the mother country would defend Canada to the utmost. He pointed out the injustice of the threat of the Americans to refuse quarter if the Indians were allowed to fight side by side with their British allies. On the 27th of July he opened an extra session of the Legislature at York (Toronto). In his address he said "by unanimity and despatch, we may teach the enemy that a country defended by freemen can never be conquered." The action of the Legislature somewhat disappointed him — for the invasion naturally produced some dispondency — the Indians in the West were known to be wavering; a portion of the population about Sandwich of French and American

extraction, and lying exposed to the first onset of the
enemy were disaffected. General Brock's strong and
hopeful attitude rallied the waverers. Inspired by his
example the country braced itself to a defence against
great odds, with a courage which may not only
excite our admiration, but gives us an example
which we at any time might be proud to follow.
Meanwhile hostilities had actually given the first
honors to Canada. General Brock had early strengthened Amherstburg on the Detroit River. He had also
seen the importance of taking possession of strategic
points of Detroit and Michilimackinac, not only to
secure the active co-operation of the Indians but also
because without them the whole of Western Canada,
perhaps even as far as Kingston would have to be
evacuated. Immediately on hearing of the declaration
of war he assumed the offensive by ordering an attack
on Michilimackinac, which was gallantly carried out
by Captain Roberts. He advanced to the attack with
45 regulars and 600 Canadians and Indians, when
the garrison capitulated. In the Amherstburg District
a little later came the success of a small British force
at Tarantee.

About the same time the famous Indian Chief
Tecumseh, captured a provision convoy of General
Hull's, along with important correspondence. Meanwhile Hull became so discouraged that he recrossed
the river to Detroit, on the 7th and 8th of August ;
on the 15th of August General Brock, after a toilsome
march from Burlington heights to Long Point on
Lake Erie and after four days and nights of hard

rowing he reached Amherstburg, with a force of 300 regulars and 400 Militia, " disguised in red coats." Here he met Tecumseh, who offered his " braves " as allies. Brock at once summoned General Hull who was in Fort Detroit to surrender, and followed this summons by the crossing of the British force. Before the assault could be carried out the garrison startled by the effects of the first fire from the batteries, surrendered to the British. By this capitulation the whole State of Michigan, a ship of war, 33 canon, stores to correspound, 2500 troops, and one stand of colors were surrendered to the British. The surrender of Detroit electrified all Canada. No more was there doubting or wavering, disaffection slunk out of sight, and Brock became the idol of Upper Canada. Leaving Procter in charge of Detroit, with as many men has he could spare, Brock hastened back to York (Toronto) on the schooner "Chippewa" hopeing now to sweep the Niagara frontier clear of every vestage of invasion, and securing Sacketts Harbor remove all danger of an attack from Lake Ontario. But on Lake Erie he was met with the news of the untimely armistice which Sir George Prevost had made with the American Gen. Dearborn. Against this armistice Brock rebelled for his hands were tied. The effect of it was to give the Americans time to repair their reverses. Meanwhile the American President did not approve of the armistice, and operations were resumed. A cordon was formed along the frontier of Lower Canada from Yamaska to St. Regis where the line of separation between the United States and Canada touches the St. Lawrence, consisting of Canadian Voltigeurs and part of the embodied Militia. A light Brigade was formed at Blainfindie, under Lt. Col. Young of the 8th Reg., and consisted of the Canadian Fencibles and the flank companies of the 8th, 100th, 103th and 1st Batt. embodied Militia.

On the Montreal frontier the road to the United States from the Camp at l'Acadie, through Odeltown was rendered impracticable by *abattis*. This work was done in a short time by the Voltigeurs, under Major de Salaberry. On the other hand the Americans under General Dearborn, threatened Montreal *via* Odeltown and St. Johns. Meanwhile the American General Van Rensellaer burning to retrieve the surrender of Detroit had concentrated on the Niagara frontier, a force of over 8,000 men. Early in October, Brock was convinced that an attack was impending, and accordingly had issued particular directions to all the posts, where a landing might be effected. A large force had collected on the American side at Lewiston, about 7 miles below the Falls. At this point the river is very narrow, and on the Canadian side was the beautiful wooded Plateau of Queenstown heights. Early on the morning of October 11, 1812 a crossing was attempted but failed owing to tempestuous weather and lack of boats. But on the 13th before day break a crossing was effected by an advance Guard of General Van Rensellaer army-protected by a Battery at every point at which they could be opposed by musketry. The landing was gallantly resisted by a small out post force of regu-

lars and Militia, backed by an 18 poundes on the
Heights, and another gun a mile below. Both assault
and resistance was resolute and brave but fresh de-
tachments of troops followed till about 1100 men
were in line confronting the British out posts. Both
Captains of the two companies of the 49th Reg. had
fallen wounded and the 18 pounder was of no avail
over a large part of the field. The engagement was
growing hot, with serious loss on both sides ; Van
Rensellaer himself being wounded. Meanwhile Brock
who was at Fort George heard the connonade, mounted his horse and galloped to the scene of action.
Before he had time to reconoiter the field, a fire was
opened in the rear from a height above a path which
had been left unguarded because reported inaccessa-
ble. This path had been gallantly scaled by a detachment of American troops. The volley was promptly
followed by a rush. Brock and his aide had no time
to remount, and were swept back with the men who
manned the Battery. A detachment of the 49th one
hundred strong, charged up the hill, and were re-
pulsed, but re-inforced charged again, and in the
struggle the whole were driven to the edge of the
bank. With a storming foe in front of them, a preci-
pice of 180 feet behind them, and the roaring river
beneath, the white flag was raised by the Americans
— but quickly torn down. Thus re-inspired by their
Commander, they opened a scathing fire. Brock who,
in front, roused beyond himself, had forgotten the
General, in the soldier, conspicious by his great
height, dress, gesture and undaunted bearing, was

pointing to the hill and had just shouted " Push on the brave York Volunteers " when he was struck by a ball in the right breast, which passed through his left side. He only lived long enough to ask that his death should be concealed from his men, and to send a message to his sister. Shortly after, McDonell his *aide-de-camp*, a Lieut.-Colonel of Militia and Attorney General for Upper Canada, while leading on the York Volunteers and breasting the hill on horseback was struck from the saddle. He was removed from the field and died next day. The great loss on both sides, now caused a lull in the fighting, the American retaining the perilous foothold they had gained at great loss, while the British retired under cover of the village awaiting reinforcements. These were already on their way. General Sheaffe, who had followed Brocks directions to collect all available troops, speedily came up with about 380 regulars, two companies of Militia, and a few Indians, re-inforced at Queenstown by more Militia and Indians, making up his total to 800 men. With this force he outflanked the enemy, and surrounded them in their dangerous position between the heights and the river. A determined onset forced them to a headlong and fearful retreat, many being dashed to pieces in descending the precipitous rocks or drowned in attempting to cross the river. The surviving remnants of the invaders, who had numbered 1,100 mustered on the brink of the river and surrendered unconditionally with their General Wadsworth, as prisoners of war. The loss on the American side was about 400 killed and

wounded. The British loss was 80 killed and wounded.
Sheaffe having thus bravely won the day was un-
fortunately led to throw away most of the advantages
of his victory by signing an armistice. For this he
is blamed by many who think he ought to have
crossed the river, and taken possession of Fort Niagara, which was fired at from Fort George and
completely dismantled and abandoned. As autumn
passed into winter, some ineffectual skirmishes occurred along the St. Lawrence. In the meantime
General Dearborn on the New York frontier of Lower
Canada had assembled an army of 10,000 men. But
the French Canadian Militia sprang to arms, the land
bristled with bayonets. Major De Salaberry, in the
infancy of his fame, had command of the outposts,
and under his inspiration these undisciplined levies
speedily showed that they were too much in ernest
to be trifled with. On the 20th of November, General Dearborn made a demonstration on a picket at
Lacolle, which consisted of Militia and a few Indians.
These were under command of Colonel Mackay,
father of the late Judge Mackay, who handled his
force so well that Dearborns force retreated to Champlain, where it took up winter quarters. The inland
American marine made in effectual attempts to capture
two British schooners, both of which escaped into
Kingston; later a small British bark became their
prize. On November 20th, Kingston was bombarded,
sustaining little damage and returned the attention
with interest. At the same time, General Smyth succeeded Van Rensaeller on the Niagara Frontier, and

made an ineffectual attempt at Fort Erie, after which
he went into winter quarters. The Legislatures of
Upper and Lower Canada met at the close of the
year and voted large sums for the equipment of the
Militia. Recruiting went on briskly during the winter,
and by spring the Canadian forces, amounted to
8,000 men, including regulars. The opposing American army, including regulars and Militia was about
27,000 strong. The campaign of 1813 opened at an ·
early date, while the frozen rivers afforded easy
passage for troops. During January, February and
March skirmishes took place along the frontier at
Amherstburg, Gananoque and Brockville. The most
important operation at the opening of the year took
place in January. An American force under General
Harrison made demonstration on Detroit which was
held by a weak garrison, under Colonel Proctor. The
season though favorable to an advance from the
American side precluded all possibility of the British
being re-inforced. On January 11th, Proctor learned
that a division under General Winchester, had been
send forward by General Harrison, and had reached
an advanced position. Proctor saw that the American force had advanced beyond the shelter of support,
so he flung his whole strength on Winchester before
Harrison could reach him. At break of day on the
22nd Proctor attacked the enemys division, about
1,000 strong, and met with a desparate resistance.
The fight continued some time, but eventually fearing
destruction of his entire force Winchester surrendered
it and himself as prisoners of war, 522 men and offi-

cers, with arms, stores and amunition, became the prize of the British — about 400 were killed and wounded. Proctor had 500 regulars and Militia and 600 Indians, and lost 180 men. For a time Detroit was secure. At Prescott, opposite Ogdensburg, a small force of some 400, principally Glengary Militia, under Colonel McDonell eagerly watching an opportumly to repay the forays which in the late autumn the Americans had made on the neighborhood of Brockville. It had been the practice since the ice had formed to drill daily on the river. Half the river belonged to them, so that they were allowed to drill and manoeuvre unmolested. On the morning of February 22nd McDonell descended on to the ice at the head of 480 men and 2 Field pieces. He played and purred for sometime with valvety touch preparing for a spring. Having divided his force into two portions, assuming himself command of one and Jenkens, a gallant New Brunswick the other, a sudden dash was made. They took the enemy completely by surprise, drove them from every position, stormed and carried the Battery, burned the barracks and 4 armed vessels frozen into the harbor, and captured eleven cannon, and a large amount of Military stores and many prisoners were taken. The American loss is placed at 75 men killed and wounded. The British loss was 8 killed and 52 wounded. For a moment or two allow one to digree from actual warefare, to explain who and what were the Glengarians, who played so important a part in this war. After the American revolution, the Counties of Stormont,

Dunday and Glengarry were appropriated by the British Government as a place of settlement for United Empire Loyalists. It so happened that among those early settlers, a majority consisted of Scotch Highlanders, the descendants of men who after Culloden, had been transported to the plantations. To them was added a gallant band of Scottish soldiers who had fought against France from 1792 to 1803. The brief peace of 1802, led to the unfortunate disbandment of many fine British Regiments, and among them a regiment of Roman Catholic Highlanders, raised only a few years before by Alexander McDonnell of Glen Urquhart, a Catholic clergyman of great energy of character. He had been appointed their chaplain. On their disbandment he obtained from the British Government the means to trensport the men of the Glengarry Regiment to Canada. He led them into the wilderness, and engrafted on the waste, their faith to God and fidelity to the throne. The ernest priest, and tried friends through life never deserted them. Partaking of the charactert of the Mediacal churchman, half Bishop, half Baron he fought and prayed, with equal zeal by the side of men whom he had come to regard as his hereditary followers. He rose to the Episcopate and died, universally belowed, Bishop of Kingston. In raising the Glengarry Regiment, he was must active in rousing the enthusiasm of his parishioners. The firy cross had passed through the land, and every clansman obeyed the summons. This is the stock which nearly one hundred years ago, and more, was placed in these counties, and which has all but retained its same exclusive character, as it has its well tried loyalty. In March 1813, the 104th " Regt." left Fredrickton to reinforce the troops in Canada. Coffin in his little work on these three years of war, says : "These men actually marched on snow shoes the entire distance between Fredrickton and the St. Lawrence, confronting hardships, to which the march of the Guards in January, 1862, was but a holiday freak. During the winter months the Americans had been exceedingly active not only in preparing troops but in preparing to obtain the supremacy of Lake Ontario. England had not even yet realised the full gravity of the situation, though the Canadians did. Indications were that Toronto, then know as York, was to be attacked. It contained a little less than 1,000 souls, and a garrison of about 600, 200 or 300 regulars, and the rest Militia. On the 25th of April Commodore Chauney and General Dearborn left Sacketts Harbor with sixteen sail and conveying a land force of 2500 men. Videttes had for some time before been on constant watch, with order to fire alarm guns, and then ride into town, on sight of a hostile fleet. It was late in the evening of April 26, when the first report hushed every voice, and for a moment startled the whole population. But the men of York paused not long, old and young rushed to arms. On the first alarm General Sheaffe got his men in hand, and awaited what the morning would bring forth. But York was incapable of defence, in fact all the troops then in Western Canada would have been insufficient. He therefore made the necessary preparation for meeting the enemy, and if hard pressed, to save his force, destroy all public property, and retire either on Burlington Heights or Kingston, according to the developements of the enemy. At early dawn the American Squadron was seen bearing down on the western flank of the town. While they engaged a small mutilated 3 gun Battery at what is known as the old fort, a large force landed and cut of all retreat westward. Sheaffe sent the best portion of his force to keep the enemy at bay. For a time the enemy were held in check, but being re-inforced in over whelming numbers, the British were outflanked and compelled to retire with a loss of nearly 100 in killed, wounded and prisoners. An accidental explosion of one of the batteries, silenced the fort guns and as this left no hope of successful resistance Sheaffe destroyed such stores as he could, and took with him such as he was able, and retreated on Kingston. Meantime the American advanced column having taken possession of the fort, were nearly destroyed by the believed accidental explosion of the magazine. Although Sheaffe left an officer to arrange terms of capitulation the Public Buildings were burned, the Church and Library pillaged and acts of vandalism perpetrated contrary to the articles of the capitulation. General Dearborn made no attempt to pursue the retreating British force. Newark now Niagara defended by General Vincent with 1,340 troops, stationed at Fort George, was the next point of attack. Contrary winds, bothered the flotilla greatly, but it reached the American shore about the 8th of May, where it lay for about two weeks, receiving reinforcements from Sacketts Harbor.

On the 27th of May, the American force now augmented to between 7 and 8,000 men, effected a landing about a mile from the fort, in spite of a very vigorous resistance from 250 Militia men, and 40 Indians. They were, however forced back upon the main body. Vincent and his men did all that brave soldiers could do to oppose the advance; but after a desperate struggle of three hours against odds, in which both officers and men suffered severely, he determined to retreat to save the remainder of his men. He left 350 regular troops and 85 Militia, killed or wounded on the ground. Fort George with guns spiked fell into the hands of the enemy. Vincent retreated upon the strong position of " Beaver Dam." Here he was reinforced from Fort Erie and Chippewa, and supported by a small force of the Royal Navy, he reached Burlington heights in safety, and established himself in a strong position, on what is now part of the City of Hamilton, to await orders from Quebec. Meantime a demonstration was made from Kingston upon Sacketts Harbor. On the same day that York fell, a half dozen large and a few smaller vessels sailed from Kingston, with 750 troops. Sacketts Harbor was reached about noon, but though no sign of resistance was visible, and the men were actually in the boats, the landing was without apparent reason abandoned, and the vessels left to hang about till two days later, when it was gallantly effected. and the

American regular troops routed and driven into their stockaded barracks and fort. Everything promised that this important stronghold would fall into the hands of the British, when Prevost, who is by nearly all writers, styled the evil genius of the Campaign, ordered a retreat, against the earnest protest of Colonel Drummond of the 10th Regt. Even the wounded, three of whom were officers, were deserted, and this though the re-embarkation took place in good order. This expedition was a shock to his reputation from which he never recovered. Though Dearborn had not showed any particular energy in following up his successes at York and Niagara, yet he felt the necessity of disloging Vincent from his position on Burlington heights. On the 5th of June, Vincent was apprised of the advance of an American force of 3,500 men, under Brigadiers Chandler and Winters. Colonel Harvey, who had just arrived, to assume the position of Deputy Adjutant General, offered to lead a night attack against the approaching force, in pursuance of his policy of " bold offensive operations." It was most successfully carried out at Stoney Creek. The enemy were taken unwares. The engagement lasted about an hour and a half, when the American army was completely demoralised. It destroyed its baggage and retreated to where the town of Grimsby now stands. The British retired at day light, in good order, with a hundred prisoners, which included Generals Chandler and Winters. Several guns were also captured. This successful attack on a force numbering five times its assailants, rallied the dis-

couraged defenders of Canada and for the time turned
the fortunes of war, saving Kingston and the Niagara
district. The American troops now thrown back on
to the edge of the frontier at Fort George, determined
to surprise the British depot at " Beaver Dam." This
attempt was frustrated by the gallant exploit, of a
brave woman, Laura Secord, wife of a Militia officer,
wounded at the battle of Queenstown Heights.
Hearing of the intended attack, she undertook a perilous journey of twenty miles through the woods, in
order to warn Fitzgibbon, the officer in command.
The timely warning which he received, enabled him
to concentrate his forces, so that with about three
score regulars and 250 Indians, he was able not only
to repulsethe attack, but also to capture the entire attacking force of 542 men, 2 field pieces two ammunition wagons, and the colors of the 14th U. S. Infantry. This brillant exploit was followed early in July by
dashing and successful sallies on Fort Schlosser and
Black Rock. In the latter, where Colonel Bishopp the
British Commander lost his life, the British burned
the Barracks, Naval Arsenal, and a fine schooner.
In the meantime things were going badly with the
British, both on Lake Erie and the Western Canada
peninsula. On the Lakes, Sir James Yeo was in
command of the Navy, but the means placed at his
disposal were utterly inadequate to enable him to
maintain that supremacy which was so essential to
the defence of Canada. On the 11th of September,
an engagement took plan between the two navies, the
preponderance being very largely in favor of the

Americans. The engagement lasted five hours, when the British surrendered, every vessel had become unmanageable, every officer killed or wounded and one third of the men wounded. On the America side, the loss was 123 killed or wounded, out of a force of 600 men. This defeat was a fatal one for General Proctor. It destroyed his last hope, and ruin or retreat seemed his only alternative. He was without supplies or necessary clothing and disease was ripe among his men. Amherstburg was practically defenceless, as it had been stripped of guns and ammunition to equip the fleet. He therefore decided upon destroying the forts at Detroit and Amherstburg and retreating on Burlington Heigts. Tecumseh and his Indians protested but finally yielded, and adhered to the falling fortunes of their Brittsh allies with noble and unwavering constancy. The retreat began on the 27th of September, and from the careless way in which it was conducted it was evident that Proctor did not expect the American force to follow him. The bridges were left standing, the men were badly and irregular lyfed, orders were absent or conflicting. The soldiers were utterly dispirited by the alsence of any plan or energy at Head Quarters and were in no condition to fight even equal numbers certainly not a vastly numerically superior force.

The American troops unencumbered, rapidly gained on Proctor's force and came up to it, two miles from a village of christian Indians, called Moraviantown. The relative strength of the forces was Americans 3,500 of whom 1,500 were mounted riflemen.

British about 500 and 890 Indians under Tecumseh. The charge of the Americans soon dispersed the small band of regulars, and though Tecumseh and his men thus left unsupported fought gallantly, they were eventually forced to give way with the loss of their noble chieftain. Only about 50 escaped, the remainder were taken prisoners. Proctor with about 250 men remaining, managed to effect his retreat to Burlington Heights. His military career was by this, the saddest reverse of the war, closed forever. It however awoke in the Canadian people a spirit of more intense and dogged resolution to defend their country to the last. On the appearance of Proctor at Burlington Heights, Vincent whose Head Quarters was some 7 miles from Fort George, broke up his camp, and joined him, determined to make a last stand in defence of the Western Peninsula, should the American force, make its appearance. Fortunately it was recalled to Detroit. Meanwhile on the Atlantic, British and American men of war had been engaged with alternate success and defeat on either side. About the same time the Americans tried to capture Isle aux Noix on the Richelieu River, 12 miles above St. Johns, but failed. This was followed by reprisals on Plattsburgh and Burlington by the British. In September a body of 8,000 men was collected at Sacketts Harbor, having in view the descent of the St. Lawrence, and the capture of Montreal. The embarkation took place on the 17th of October, and consisted of four Brigades. This was known at Kingston in a few hours, whence 8 gun boats, and a Mili-

tary force of 900 men and 3 field pieces, followed the
American flotilla. The American force landed near
Prescott, and continued their march along the shore,
their boats cruising close to American side. The General commanding the American troops was named
Wilkinson, whose character and sobriety is bitterly
attacked. Lt. Colonel Morrison of the 89th was in
command of the troops sent from Kingston in pursuit. He debarked his troops at Iroquois, and continued
the pursuit by land. On the 11th November he
came up to Boyd division of 2,500 men and six field
guns at a point half way between Morrisburg and
Aultsville, known a Chryslers farm, and considering
the site advantageous, offerred battle. Wilkinson
seems to have supposed that Boyds division would
alone, be sufficient to meet the British. The engagement began shortly after two o'clock, and was exceedingly sharp. By 5 o'clock, the Americans were in full
retreat, in fact were fast becoming a disorderly rout
when a re-inforcement of 600 men arrived, too late
to do more than give confidence and safety to the
flying troops, who took to their boats and hid their
flight in the darkness of that November night. The
looses were British 22 killed, 157 wounded, 12 missing; Americans killed 102, wounded 237. About 100
prisoners were taken but there was no attempt at pursuit, the British being worn out with fatigue, and
having neither cavalery or reserve. The day previous
to this battle, Wilkinson had sent forward to Cornwall
to sieze the government stores, a division of over
3,000 men under General Brown. In the meantime

Lt. Colonel Morrison continued his advance. On the 12th November, the main American army formed a junction with Brown's division, and about sunset on this day he heard of the defeat of Hamptons force at Chateauguay. He at once determined to relinquish the proposed attack on Montreal, and began his retreat. He sailed with his flotilla up the Salmon river and went into winter quarters at French Mills, now Fort Covington. Here sickness and famine preyed upon his men until February, when boats and barracks were burned and the place abandoned, part of the force going back to Sacketts Harbor, while Wilkinson led the remainder to Platsburgh.

The importance and effect of this engagement cannot be over estimated. It was "the battle of Montreal" says one writer. By diverting the expedition from this city it completely frustrated every object for which it was formed. For a mere handful of men to defeat the largest hostile army that has ever set foot on Canadian soil, added greatly to the prestige of British and Canadian arms. We now turn to Eastern Canada, now the Province of Quebec, and for a few moments I desire to allude to the part the Roman Catholic Clergy played in this war. The head of the church was the Rev. Father Plessis, Bishop of Quebec, and born in Montreal in 1763. He was intensly loyal the British Crown. In an address, which the made at the opening of the war he said : " In considering the vexatious tricks organised against the church and people of Canada, by chiefs who were sent from the Court of

Louis the 14" he frankly admitted that under the English Government, the Catholic Clergy and rural population enjoyed more liberty than was acceded to them before the conquest. After having praised the English Nation which he said had generously welcomed the French ecclesiastics, hunted out of France by the Republicans of 1792, he added "that the capitulation as well as the treaty of 1763 were so many new ties of attachment to Great Britain and that religion itself would gain by the change of domination." Holding such sentiment he issued an episcopal *mandement*, which was read in every church. In it he said " it is to you belongs the task of opposing yourselves like a wall to the approach of the enemy. They will cease to be formidable, when the God of battles fights on your side, under his holy protection, march to combat, as to victory. Sustain your reputation for obedience, for discipline, for valour, for intrepidity. Your confidence will not be vain, if in exposing your lives for the defence of your country and your hearths, you take care before all things to make your peace with God." These sentiments of the Bishop were enforced with earnetness by the clergy every where, and the result was that recruiting was most successful. On the 22nd of September 1813, Hampton, who was in command on Lake Champlain entered Canada at Odelltown, with 5,000 men. Finding his avance opposed by the outposts of DeSalaberry, he retraced his steps and made a fresh advance by the roads leading northerly to Chateauguay. DeSalaberry with a force of 300 Canadian troops advanced to oppose him at Chateauguay, where he fortified his position with a block house and an *abattis*. Here he was unexpectedly re-inforced by McDonnell of the Ogdensburgh force. On the 28th of October two columns of the enemy 7000 strong, advanced from opposite points with the intention of surrounding and crushing the Canadians. It is needless, in fact impossible for me to enter into details of the fight. I would say however that when the first line of the Voltigeurs was driven back, De Salaberry remained with a small drummer boy, who continued sounding the advance. McDonnell also by an adroit disposition of the buglers in the woods, sounding the advance at great distances apart, induced the foe to believe that a numerous force was advancing in different directions, while a few Indians, who were in the Canadian force, added to their dismay, by hideous yells. The result was that the American column broke and fled leaving, the field and the honors of the day to the little force which with two or three exceptions, was entirely French Canadian. Among the French Canadian officers severely wounded, was Capt. de Bartach, whose daughter married the late judge Monk, and is the mother of the present member in the Dominion Parliament for Jacques-Cartier. This brilliant exploit completely frustrated the projected attack on Montreal by the combined forces of Hampton and Wilkinson.

Meanwhile Harrison's troops had been pillaging the settlers in the neighborhood of Fort George. He was succeeded by McClure who continued his policy of driving the peaceful inhabitants from their homes. Colonel Murray with 378 of the 100th Regt. and a few Indians and Volunteers, advanced against him with a view of checking his operations. McClure retreated and was followed by Murray to the immediate vicinity of Fort George. He then determined to retire to the American side. Before doing so he burned the village of Niagara, only giving an hour's notice, thus leaving 400 women and children houseless on a cold December evening. Murray at once seized Fort George. The Americans left behind them a number of heavy guns which they had mounted, magazines of shot and ammunition, and camp equipage for 4,500 men. Murray then determined to cross the river, and by a night attack capture the American Fort Niagara. The expedition landed on the American shore, 3 miles above the fort at 4 o'clock, on a very dark December morning. The advance was quickly made, and when the fort was reached it was surprised by a bayonet charge and captured. With a loss of only 6 killed and 5 wounded the British captured a fort, mounting 17 guns, took 318 prisoners captured 3,000 stand of arms and large quantities of commissariat stores. The Royal Scots and the 41st Regt. under Drummond and Riall, pushed on and took Black Rock after a sharp contest. They pursued the American militia to Buffalo, which was captured and burned. The British retired and on their way burned the village of Black Rock, as a retribution for the burning of Niagara by McClure. As the result of this foray the British left the whole American frontier from Lake Ontario to Lake Erie a desolate scene of ruin. Thus the campaign of 1813 closed with the preponderance of success largely on the side of the British and Canadian forces. The invaders had not yet secured a position on Canadian soil, with the exception of Amherstburg, for the loss of which, more than an equivalant had been gained by the possession of Fort Niagara. On the other hand the Americans with their seaboard blockaded by British men of war, their commerce paralysed, their taxation increased, felt that the war they had forced upon Canada was pressing severely on themselves. The campaign of 1814 was opened by the American army under Wilkinson, advancing, on the 17th March, from Plattsburg, on the village of Champlain with a force of 4,000 men. A brigade, under General Macomb, was thrown into Swanton and then took possession of the village of Phillipsburg, a mile within Canadian territory, but soon rejoined the main body which advanced on March 30th, against Lacolle Mill. This was a small stone building on the Lacolle River, with a shingle roof, and defended by extemporised wooden windows barred by beams and loopholed for musketry. It was garrisoned by about 180 men, and its capture was considered so certain that a detachment was sent to the rear to cut off the escape of the defenders. Just as the engagement commenced a reinforcement of two companies of the 13th arrived from Isle aux Noix, after a terrible march through slush, often wading through water up to their knees. This brought the total British force up to

340 men. A bridge that crossed the Lacolle river, below the Mill, led to a small house, which by means of logs, made into a breast work, was converted into a block-house. With the exception of a small clearance, these buildings were surrounded by woods. There was a foot of snow on the ground. The Lacolle River was still frozen to within a short distance of its junction with the Richelieu. The attack began at half past one, by an attempt to flank several pieces of artillery, but after repeated trials was abandoned. Later it was renewed and a 12 pounder, a 5 pounder and a five and a half pound howitzer got into position, when a cannonade of the mill began, which was briskly replied to by musketry. This was continued for several hours, during which the two companies of the 13th stationed in the woods, several times charged the guns, but eventually were compelled to retire into the block-house. During one of these charges, the American artillerymen were forced from their guns, but the odds were too great for anything of this kind being more than a temporary success. Though the mill was struck several times and somewhat damaged, though the ammunition was scarce there was no sign of surrender. Dark coming on the fight ceased, and the American force retired. The British commander could not understand this movement. Although he felt the strength of the force which attacked him, he could scarcely have conceived that it was 4,000 strong. He therefore remained on guard all night, as he thought the movement was a feint to draw him from his position. Expecting an attack in

the morning, he, during the night, brought up from the gun-boats, frozen in the river, two 18 lb. carronades which he posted at the block-house. With the coming morning there was no enemy in sight. The truth is the United States forces were exhausted by the cold and fatigue. Morever they thought that without heavy artillery the place was impregnable. In the condition of the roads, such guns could not be brought forward. The entire American force retired to Champlain, and later the major part was ordered to Plattsburg. The British loss was 11 rank and file killed, 2 officers 1 sergeant and 43 rank and file wounded, and 4 missing, one Indian killed and one wounded. The loss on the part of the United States forces was 13 killed 128 wounded 13 missing. In the meantime the British force on this frontier, at St. John and Isle aux Noix, had been raised to about 1,000 regular troops and 450 Militia. They were however kept entirely on the defensive and the Americans were allowed to proceed in the work at Vergennes, on two vessels. So satisfied were they that an attack was intended by the British, that 500 men were brought thither from Plattsburg for their protection. When they had been launched however, Capt. Pring with two small gun-boats made a demonstration against them, which being unsupported by a land force turned out a failure. Prevost, is held responsible for this. He likewise refused to allow Sir George Drummond to attack Sackett's Harbor which was considered necessary, to break the power, of the Americans on Lake Ontario. He was however, induced by him to agree to an attack on Oswego, which had a well defended fort. It was from this place in 1760 that Amherst sailed down the St. Lawrence, landed at Lachine, marched into Montreal, camped on the site of the priests farm on Sherbrooke street and took possession of Montreal. The British fleet, consisting of 2 frigates, six others vessels and eleven gun-boats, and carrying 1,080 soldiers sailed from Kingston on the 4th of May and on the morning of the 6th the troops were successfully landed under a hot fire from the batteries, and the discharge of 500 muskets. Advancing steadily up the hill under this destructive fire, the British gained the summit to find the defence abandoned, and the defenders in flight. Within 10 minutes from their entry the Union Jack was raised on the flag staff amid the enthusiastic cheers of the soldiers. The British lost 19 killed and 62 wounded, among the former were 2 officers and among the latter 6 officers. The Americans lost 6 killed, 38 wounded and 23 missing. Sixty prisoners were taken. Nine guns and several craft, with large stores of provisions were captured of and a large quantity of ammunition destroyed and the barracks burned. Chauncey, in command of the American fleet on Lake Ontario, was next blockaded at Sacket's Harbor, and part of his expected supplies intercepted by gun-boats, though an attempt to pursue a convoy, retreating into a creek in that neighborhood, ended in defeat, with heavy loss and the surrender of 120 men.

The chief interest in the campaign now again

shifts to the West. In May an American force of
1,500 men made a descent on Port Dover, defended
by a troop of dragoons and a few militia, who were
driven away. The town was then burned to the
ground. Meanwhile large bodies of American
troops were being, during May and June, massed at
Buffalo, under Col. Winfield Scott. The force consisted of two brigades of 2,200 men each, also 500
artillery, while between Buffalo and Lewiston was
a regiment of infantry and some rifles, making a
total force of a little more than 5,000 men. To
oppose this force the British had about 4,500 men,
consisting of 1st Batt. Royal Scots, 8th, 41st, 100th,
103rd and a squadron of the 19th dragoons. From
this limited strength, garrisons had to be supplied to
Fort Erie, opposite Buffalo, Fort Niagara on the
United States side, captured the previous November,
also Fort George and the newly-constructed Fort Mis-
sisaga, at the mouth of the Niagara River. More-
over, the American navy held supremacy on Lake
Erie, and it was within the possibilities that a force
might be landed on its shores and marched across
the country. A force was therefore stationed at
Port Dover, and at another post established in the
vicinity of the present city of London. The post at
Burlington Heights had also to be defended. Sir
Geo. Drummond watched the preparations at Buffalo
with great anxiety. He saw the magnitude of the
attempt that would be made, and the necessity of
Canada meeting it as strongly as possible. He asked
Prevost that reinforcements be sent him from East-

ern Canada, as he thought the gathering of a force
at Plattsburg was only a feint, but he was refused.
Drummond felt that the blow might fall at any moment, and being uncertain as to where the landing
would be made, had distributed his force at various
points. On the 3rd of July, at day break, the American army crossed the river—one division a mile and
a half above Fort Erie, the other division a short
distance below. A heavy fog concealed their move-
ments. Fort Erie was poorly fortified and held by
100 men, who surrendered and were made prisoners.
They then pushed on to Chippewa, where Pearson
was in command with 700 regulars, 300 militia and
300 Indians. Pearson at first advanced, but finding
the Americans in force, retreated, destroying the
bridges behind him. He was followed, however,
the bridges being rapidly repaired. Riall, who was
entrenched about two miles in the rear, near Street's
Creek, heard about 8 a.m. of the American advance.
He at once ordered five companies of the Royal
Scots to join his forces. He had previously sent
word to York to have the 8th regiment join him.
On the morning of the 4th of July Scott's brigade of
the American army advanced toward Chippewa,
Riall being in his entrenchments. On the morning
of the 5th he received reinforcements, bringing his
force up to 1,500 regulars, some militia and Indians.
At 4 p.m. he advanced against the Americans.
Kingsford in his magnificent "History of Canada"
calls this action the "Balaclava" of the campaign.
Again and again the British charged against the

solid American line, and were as often forced back by a terrific shower of grape, cannon and musketry. As fast as men fell the line closed up. When the British were within 80 yards the line got into confusion, and Riall seeing the terrible slaughter, and that success was impossible, withrew his men, the 8th Regiment covering the retreat. This was carried out most orderly, not a gun or a prisoner falling into the enemy's hands. The loss of the American troops is put at 308 killed, wounded and missing, but it is believed to have been much heavier. The British lost one-third of the men taken into action, viz., 149 killed, 316 wounded, 46 missing—a total of 511. Of this number the Royal Scots lost 63 killed and 135 wounded, and the 100th 70 killed and 134 wounded. Among the officers of the 100th severely wounded was the Marquis of Tweedale. No immediate attempt was made by the United States troops to follow up their success. Riall destroyed his entrenchments and retreated along the Niagara River to Fort George, within which he took refuge. The American army advanced leisurely, with much caution, and took possession of Queenstown heights. Here it remained nearly inactive for some time. It however made marauding excursions in various directions, some of which were attacked by the British, many prisoners being taken. General Brown, of the American army, had been expecting the assistance of Chauncy's fleet to enable him to take Fort George, but owing partly to the illness of Chauncy and partly to the fact that he was

now effectually held in check by the British fleet of
Yeo. Brown, gave up his design on the fort, and retreated towards Chippewa, closely followed by Riall,
who took up an advantageous position on a rising
ground in a country road called Lundy's Lane,
while a waiting reinforcements. Meanwhile Drummond at Kingston, on hearing of the action at Street's
Creek, had ordered a new levy of the militia of the
province, and a number of them, who had returned
temporarily to their farms, loyally responded to the
call. Drummond hastened on to York (Toronto),
and with 400 men of the 89th and other companies,
he pushed on to Niagara. Finding that Riall had
already advanced, he sent a detachment under Col.
Tucker, against an American force at Lewiston,
while he himself pushed on to Queenstown. The
enemy having disappeared from Lewiston, Tucker
re-crossed the river with his detachment and Drummond's re-united column of 800 men, advanced to
join Riall's of about the same number. Meanwhile
Winfield Scott, believing that the British force opposed to him at Lundy's Lane, was greater than he
at first thought, sent for reinforcements, and Gen.
Brown, with Ripley's and Foster's brigades, hastened to his support. Riall finding that he was about
to be attacked by an overwhelming force, had commenced a retreat, when Drummond arrived and
countermanded it. He found himself in command
of 1,600 men, and confronted by an American force
of at least 5,000 men, part of which had advanced
to within 600 yards by the time he had reached the

top of the hill at Lundy's Lane. The engagement
began with an attack from Scott's brigade before
Riall had completed his formation, though he lost no
time in establishing a battery of two guns on a small
eminence. Today from thence, on a summer day,
the eye can take in a large expanse of sunny, peaceful country, rich woodlands, peach orchards and
vineyards, tranquil homesteads and fields of living
green. But on that July evening, from six o'clock
till midnight, the peaceful landscape was clouded
with heavy sulphurous smoke, the sweet summer air
was filled with the dull boom of artillery and the rattle
of musketry, the shout of the charge, the groans of the
wounded, all blending strangely with the solemn,
unceasing roar of the great cataract close by. The
battle, the most fiercely contested of the whole war,
raged with fierce obstinacy and severe carnage, and
an obstinate determination on both sides. About 9
o'clock a brief lull in the fighting occurred, while the
rear guard of the American force under Gen. Brown
took the place of Scott's brigade, which had suffered
severely. At this critical moment Sir Hercules Scott,
with 1,200 men, arrived on the spot after a march of
twenty-one miles, and between the two unequal
forces thus re-inforced the British resumed the contest. The chief struggle was for the possession of
the guns on the height. By a successful dash at
one time of the Americans they were for a time
taken, but were soon retaken. The darkness was
so great that in a retreat two guns were exchanged.
Nothing, says an on-looker, could have been more

terrible, nor yet more solemn, than this midnight contest. The desperate charges of the Americans was succeded by a death-like silence, interrupted only by the groans of the dying and the dull roar of the falls of Niagara. About midnight Brown, having unsuccessfully, for six hours, with his force of 5,000 men, against little more than half that number, tried to force the British from their position, retreated to Chippewa with a loss of 930, that on the British side amounting to 870. Riall had been wounded and taken prisoner early in the action, and both Scott and Brown were wounded, Scott having had two horses shot under him. Drummond was badly wounded in the neck, but retained his command untill the end of the battle, cheerily urging on his men to fight to the last. On the next morning, the 26th, the American commander, having destroyed the bridge over the Chippewa, burned Street's Mill and thrown much of his equipage and provisions into the river, retired to Fort Erie, which had been greatly strengthened since it surrendered to the Americans. Drummond having received reinforcements was now in command of 3,150 men—the garrison at Fort Erie numbering 3,000. On the 1st of August he moved his headquarters to midway between Chippewa and Fort Erie. On the following day he moved to opposite Black Rock, from which point he sent a detachment of some seven hundred men across the river, with the intention of taking Buffalo and thus cutting off the supplies from Fort Erie. The expedition found itself strongly opposed, and was, after a severe engagement, forced to retire with considerable loss. He then made a gallant attempt to capture Fort Erie, which was partially successful, but, just as the first column had entered the *embrasures*, an accidental explosion killed many of the storming party. This caused a panic which compelled Drummond to retire with a loss of more than 500 men. Being reinforced by the 32nd and 61st Regiments, Drummond entrenched himself and waited developments. On the 17th of September Brown, with a large force, attacked the British entrenchments. The fighting began at 2 o'clock in the afternoon and was continued till 5 o'clock. In the early part of the battle the British were forced from their entrenchments, but soon recaptured them and drove the Americans back. They then retired upon Fort Erie. The defeat of this attack was so severely felt that no attempt was made to renew it. The severity of the fighting will be understood from the losses, viz: British, 115 killed, 178 wounded; United States, 80 killed, 214 wounded. Meanwhile reenforcement of 16,000 men from England had arrived, and Prevost, assisted by a fleet on Lake Champlain and an army of some 10,000 or 12,000 men, made an attack on Plattsburgh, and met with an inglorious defeat, which, it is admitted, was a surprise to themselves. Kingsford says that the Americans had made every arrangement to evacuate the place, so satisfied were they that the British would be successful. A large body of the troops at Plattsburgh had been sent to reinforce the blockading troops on

Lake Erie, leaving General Macomb with only 1,500 militia, newly called out. Prevost might easily have overpowered his weak enemy, but he was obstinately determined to await the attack of the newly collected fleet commanded by Downie, who was almost a stranger to his command, and who was prematurely hurried into action by Prevost. Downie was killed 15 minutes after the firing began, and the British vessels were overpowered. Instead of attacking simultaneously with his artillery, he waited till the fleet had been defeated by the greatly superior squadron opposed to him, when he countermanded the advance of the troops he had so irresolutely put in motion, and ordered a retreat without even an attempt at an assault. The indignation of the disappointed troops was almost uncontrollable, and Macomb could hardly believe his good fortune. For the lamentable incompetency manifested in his conduct of this affair Prevost was to have been tried by court martial, but died before this could take place.

The end of this long and exhausting war was happily near at hand. The close of the general war in Europe early in 1814 had left Great Britain free to begin a retaliatory naval war on the United States, the effects of which were soon felt. The American seaboard, from Maine to Mexico, suffered from the inroads of British squadrons, whose attacks forced the recall of a portion of the American land forces then in Canada. Sir John Sherbrooke, Lieutenant Governor of Nova Scotia, made successful attacks on the coast of Maine, carrying one point

after another, till the whole border, from Penobscot
to New Brunswick, was under British rule, and so
continued till the ratification of peace. About the
middle of August, Admiral Cockburn, with 50 vessels, arrived at Chesapeake Bay with troops destined
for the attack on Washington. Tangier Island was
seized and fortified, and 1.500 negroes belonging to
neighboring plantations were armed and drilled.
There were two rivers by which Washington might
be approached: the Potomac, on which it is situated, and the Patuxen, which flows in its rear. The
British commander chose the latter, both on account of the facility of access and for the purpose of
destroying the powerful fleet of gunboats which had
taken refuge in its creeks. This object was successfully accomplished on the 20th of August, 15 of the
gunboats being destroyed and one captured, together
with 14 merchant vessels. The army was under
the command of General Ross, and the following
day disembarked at Benedict. It numbered, including
some Royal marines, 3,500 men, with two hundred
sailors to drag the guns — two small three-pounders.
For the defence of Washington, General Winder had
been assigned 16,600 regulars, and a levy of 93,000
militia had been ordered. Of the latter not one put
in an appearance, and of the former only about half
had reached the Capital. The Americans had, however, 26 guns to oppose the two which the British
had with them. General Winter took up a position
at Bladensburg, a few miles from Washington. His
batteries commanded the only bridge across the East
Potomac. General Ross determined to storm the

bridge in two columns.   Not a moment did the veterans of the Peninsular war hesitate.   Amid a storm of shot and shell they dashed across the bridge, carried a fortified house, and charged on the batteries before the second column could come to their aid. Ten guns were captured.   The American army was utterly routed, and fled through and beyond the city it was to defend.   The lack of cavalry and the intense heat prevented pursuit by the British, who lost sixteen men killed and 185 wounded.   Towards evening the British occupied Washington.   The destruction of the public buildings had been decreed, in retaliation for the pillage of York (Toronto) and the wanton burning of Niagara.   Writing of this episode of the war, Kingsford says :   " For over two years the United States had conducted war on Canada with the spirit of ferocity.   They had commenced, without provocation, by burning the Houses of Legisture at York.   A more wanton act than the destruction by fire of Niagara is not to be found in the annals of war.   It was therefore but just that the people of the United States should themselves experience the calamities they had inflicted.   An offer was made by the United States of a large money ramson, but it was refused.   The next day the torch was applied to the Capitol, with its valuable library, the President's house, the Treasury building, the War Office arsenal, dock yard and the long bridge across the Potomac.   A fine frigate, a 20-gun sloop, 20,000 stand of arms and immense magazines of powder, had already been destroyed.   In the meantime Alexandria, on the right of the Potomac, seven miles south of Washington, had been captured by Sir James Gordon. It was saved from destruction by the surrender of 21 vessels, 16,000 barrels of flour and a thousand hogsheads of tobacco. A few days later General Ross evacuated Washington, and retired unmolested to his ships. Baltimore was next visited. On the 11th of September the fleet arrived at the mouth of the Patapsco. On the 12th General Ross landed with 3,270 troops. An advance was made; in going alone to bring forward some troops, he was shot at and killed. Col. Brooke, of the 44th regiment, assumed command. Five miles from Baltimore the British came upon the United States troops, and an engagement ensued. They — the Americans — were routed and retreated toward the city, the British bivouacking on the ground which had been held by the American troops. On the 15th the British advanced to within two mile sof Baltimore, from whence the entrenchments prepared for its defence were visible. There he remained to obtain intelligence from the fleet, and to arrange for its co-operation in storming the place. It was however found that, owing to the entrance to the harbor being obstructed by sunken ships, co-operation was impossible. Both commanders were of opinion, keeping in view their instructions, that the advantages to be gained, would not be a sufficient equivalent for the loss which might probably be experienced in storming the place. The British therefore withdrew, and like at Washington, were allowed to re-embark without molestation. In Florida the British established themselves for some time, but were de-

feated before New Orleans. Later in the year, some
hostilities of minor importance took place on Lake
Ontario, the Niagara frontier and the Western
Peninsula. In December, 1814, the British and
American envoys, who had been in session in
Ghent for some months, ratified a treaty of peace.
Thus closed this most unjustifiable war. The Rev.
Dr. Withrow summarises the situation at this time
as follows: "The calm verdict of history found
much ground for extenuation in the revolt of
1776, but for the American declaration of war in
1812, little or none. A reckless Democratic majority
wantonly invaded the country of an unoffending
neighbor, to seduce them from lawful allegiance and
annex their territory. The long and costly conflict
was alike bloody and barren. The Americans did
not annex a single foot of territory. They did not
gain a single permanent advantage. Their exposed
seaboard was attacked at every point, their capital
city destroyed, their annual exports reduced from
£22,000,000 to £1,500,000, three thousand of their vessels captured, two thirds of their commercial men became insolvent. A vast war tax was incurred, and the
very existence of the United States imperilled by
the menaced secession of the New England States.
The right of search and the right of neutrals, the
ostensible, but *not* the real cause of the war, were
not even mentioned in the treaty of peace. Many
of the leading American statesmen believed then, as
some believe even now, that the conquest of Canada
would be an easy matter." Thomas Jefferson, in
1812, just previous to the war, wrote as follows:

" The acquisition of Canada this year, as far as the neighborhood of Quebec, will be a mere matter of marching, and will give us experience for the attack on Halifax and the final expulsion of England from the American continent." At the same time Dr. Eustis, Secretary of State for War, said in Congress: "We can take Canada without soldiers; we have only to send officers into the provinces, and the people will rally round our standard." The celebrated Henry Clay, at the same time, expressed himself as follows: "It is absurd to suppose we shall not succeed in our enterprise against the enemy's provinces. We have the Canadas as much under our command as Great Britain has the ocean. I would take the whole continent from them, and ask them no favors. I wish never to see a peace till we do." Miss Machar, in the Canadian Encyclopedia, says: " To Canada the war was, from a material stand point of view, an almost unqualified misfortune; devastated territory, neglected farms, sacrificed lives and desolated homes, were long evident marks of the invasion. Forced into hostilities simply in virtue of her being an integral part of the British Empire, Canada never wavered in her loyalty, though often contending at a disadvantage against overwhelming odds. During nearly the whole duration of the war, inadequate military forces, insufficient supplies of provisions and materials of war, increased the inequality of the contest, while the incapacity of the Governor General, and at times the insufficiency of leaders, repeatedly betrayed the British cause. Yet the loyal Canadian yeomen, willingly threw themselves into the breach and fought gallantly for their homes and their flag. In moral benefit to Canada, the war was most fruitful. It gave unity and *esprit de corps* to its diverse elements. French Canadians and British Canadians fought side by side and vied with each other in devotion to their common country. Increased self respect and self reliance, fitted and educated the colony, for the responsible government it was before many years to enjoy. Many settlers were attracted to Canada, among them many military veterans, who, by the traditions they carried with them, rivetted still stronger the links to the mother land. The opening national life of the country was ennobled by its suffering for the cause it deemed the right, and strengthened, elevated and purified by its sacrifices in resisting an unrighteous invasion, it emerged from its 'baptism of fire' all the more fitted to become a noble and vigorous nation. The lot into which its struggling infancy refused to be forced, is not likely ever to become the choice of its vigorous prime."

WORKS CONSULTED. Kingsford History of Canada, Coffin's War of 1812-14, Canadian Encyclopedia, Various Pamphlets of Historical Societies.